I. C. NOEL

Top 5 Books for Leadership

Master the Art of Influence: The Definitive Guidebook to Elevate Your Leadership

First edition

This book was professionally typeset on Reedsy.
Find out more at reedsy.com

Contents

Introduction   1

"The Art and Science of Leadership" by Afsaneh Nahavandi   3

"5 Levels of Leadership" by John C Maxwell   6

"Extreme Ownership" by Jocko Willink and Leif Babin   14

"Start with Why" by Simon Sinek   20

"The Five Dysfunctions of a Team" by Patrick Lencioni   25

Conclusion   31

References   33

Introduction

L eadership is the cornerstone of progress. In organizations, communities, and nations, it's the leaders who chart the course and steer the ship through uncharted waters. This book begins with that premise: leadership matters. Its impact is profound and pervasive, and mastering it is not an option but a necessity for those who aim to excel and inspire.

The need for continuous learning in leadership cannot be overstated. Like any craft, leadership requires study, reflection, and a relentless pursuit of growth. Reading is the vessel for such growth—a direct line to the minds of history's greatest leaders, thinkers, and innovators. Through their insights and experiences, you can shape your approach, refine your strategies, and fortify your philosophy.

This book is a compass to navigate the vast sea of leadership literature. The right books can redefine your understanding of leadership and your approach to challenges. They can transform your thinking, broaden your perspective, and equip you with the tools to lead more effectively. Each book covered here has been chosen for its ability to contribute to this transformation, offering timeless wisdom applicable to the ever-evolving demands of leadership.

As you turn these pages, prepare to embark on a journey of discovery. The insights within will challenge you to think differently, act boldly, and lead with renewed purpose and vision. Welcome to a pivotal step in your leadership journey. Welcome to the definitive guide to books that will not only inform you but also transform you.

"The Art and Science of Leadership" by Afsaneh Nahavandi

Effective leadership is a harmonious blend of the precision inherent in science and the fluidity found in art, culminating in a symphony of success. This chapter delves into the dual nature of leadership, dissecting its scientific and artistic elements to provide a comprehensive understanding of what constitutes effective leadership.

At the heart of effective leadership lies a scientific approach, one that emphasizes skills, knowledge, and behavior as the pillars of leadership excellence. This triad forms the structural framework upon which successful leadership is built and sustained.

Leadership skills are the tools that enable leaders to navigate the complexities of their roles effectively. These include planning, which involves setting goals and mapping out strategies to achieve them; problem-solving, the ability to identify issues and devise effective solutions; decision-making, which requires assessing situations and making informed choices; communication, the art of conveying ideas and fostering understanding; and conflict resolution, the skill to address and resolve disputes constructively. Mastery of these skills allows leaders to guide their teams efficiently and overcome the myriad challenges they encounter.

Knowledge serves as the foundation of leadership. It encompasses an in-depth understanding of the organization's goals, ensuring that a leader's actions and decisions are aligned with the overarching vision. It also includes awareness of the organization's culture, which is crucial in shaping a positive and productive workplace environment. Additionally, knowledge of market conditions equips leaders to navigate the ever-changing business landscape effectively, while an understanding of relevant laws and regulations ensures that the organization operates within legal and ethical boundaries. This comprehensive knowledge base is critical for making strategic decisions and guiding the organization toward success.

A leader's behavior significantly impacts their leadership style and the response it elicits from the team. It is the tangible manifestation of a leader's approach, reflecting their values, beliefs, and attitudes. Consistent, positive behavioral patterns are instrumental in building trust, fostering respect, and creating an environment where team members feel valued and motivated. A leader's behavior sets the tone for the workplace culture, influencing team dynamics, morale, and overall performance. It is through their behavior that leaders model the standards they expect from their team, shaping the collective identity and driving the organization's success.

In essence, the science of leadership is about mastering a set of skills, building a robust knowledge base, and exhibiting behaviors that inspire and propel teams forward. It is a systematic and methodical approach that underpins effective leadership, enabling leaders to make informed decisions, foster positive relationships, and drive organizational success.

While the science of leadership is rooted in tangible skills and knowledge, the art of leadership delves into the more nuanced realms of emotional intelligence and intuition. These aspects of leadership, though less quantifiable, are equally crucial in shaping a leader's effectiveness and influence.

Emotional intelligence is the ability to understand and manage one's own emotions, as well as those of others. It is a pivotal component of leadership that enables leaders to connect with their team members on a deeper, more empathetic level. This connection fosters a positive work environment where trust, morale, and collaboration thrive. Leaders with high emotional intelligence are adept at recognizing and addressing the emotional needs of their team, thereby boosting motivation and engagement. They excel in communicating effectively, resolving conflicts with sensitivity, and building strong, resilient teams. Emotional intelligence also plays a vital role in helping leaders navigate through high-pressure situations with composure, maintaining a clear and focused mind to make sound decisions.

Intuition in leadership refers to the instinctive understanding or insight that guides decision-making, especially in situations where historical data or precedent may be lacking. It is the leader's inner compass, often drawing upon a subconscious synthesis of their experience, knowledge, and observation. Leaders who trust and hone their intuition often find themselves at the forefront of innovation and strategy. They are able to read between the lines of complex situations, making informed and sometimes unconventional decisions that can lead to groundbreaking outcomes. Intuitive leaders are characterized by their ability to anticipate trends, seize opportunities, and mitigate risks, often before these become apparent to others.

The art of leadership, encompassing emotional intelligence and intuition, complements the more structured and analytical approach of its scientific counterpart. It brings a human touch to leadership, emphasizing the importance of understanding and relating to people, and trusting one's instincts in guiding actions and decisions. This blend of emotional depth and intuitive insight is what transforms a good leader into a truly great one, enabling them to inspire, influence, and lead with both heart and mind.

"5 Levels of Leadership" by John C Maxwell

I n the quest for effective leadership, one navigates through the stratified layers of influence and authority. John C. Maxwell, in his insightful work, delineates these strata into five distinct levels—each serving as a stepping stone to the zenith of leadership prowess.

Position – The Foundational Step

Position is the bedrock of leadership, the first and most accessible rung on the ladder of influence. It is often handed over like a baton in a relay—attached to a title or role within an organization—and comes with a predefined measure of authority. This level is where leadership begins, not through personal influence but through the conferred power of a title.

The ease with which a position can be attained often belies its importance. For many, it is the culmination of academic or professional milestones, an entry point that validates expertise or tenure. However, the very accessibility of positional leadership makes it a double-edged sword. It is straightforward because it is systematic, often a result of hierarchy rather than personal merit.

Yet, despite its apparent simplicity, positional leadership is foundational for a reason. It provides the platform from which one can embark on the journey of becoming a true leader. It is a place of potential power, where the opportunity to guide and direct is immediately present.

But it is a precarious base, for the authority it grants is superficial at best. Followership at this level is compulsory rather than voluntary. People follow because they must, not because they choose to, and their allegiance is to the position, not to the person who holds it.

This level's shallowness stems from its dependency on the title and the systemic power structure. It does not require the leader to be particularly skilled at influencing others; it simply requires them to fill a slot. The true test of leadership does not reside in the mere occupancy of a position but in the ability to transcend it. The goal of the positional leader should be to build legitimacy, to transform the provisional authority of their role into genuine leadership currency. The leader at this level must recognize the limitations of their position and strive to create a deeper connection with their team—a connection that extends beyond the superficiality of titles and taps into the reservoir of authentic influence.

Permission – The Relational Rung

The transition from Position to Permission is a pivotal evolution in the leadership journey. Permission is the level where a leader's influence expands from the mandatory to the discretionary. It is no longer the title that wields power; it is the leader's personal attributes—trust, integrity, and respect—that become the source of their influence.

At this juncture, leadership transforms from a role to a relationship. Unlike the Position level, where subordinates follow because they have to, at the Permission level, they follow because they want to. This shift occurs as the leader begins to engage with their team on a more personal level, seeing and treating them as individuals with their aspirations and needs.

To move from Position to Permission, a leader must demonstrate a genuine interest in the well-being of their team members. It involves active listening, empathy, and a commitment to understanding the personal drivers of each team member. A leader at this level invests time in building trust and rapport, which is the currency of Permission.

The leader who operates on Permission makes people feel valued, not merely as cogs in a machine but as essential contributors to the team's vision. Communication is two-way; feedback is encouraged and acted upon. This engenders a sense of ownership and commitment among team members, leading to a more collaborative and energized environment.

Leaders can facilitate their move from Position to Permission by consistently respecting others' opinions, sharing credit for successes, and promoting an inclusive team culture. It's about shifting the focus from commanding to connecting, from wielding power to empowering. Leaders at this level understand that the strength of their influence is directly proportional to the strength of their relationships. By granting their followers permission to take ownership of their roles, leaders not only enhance their influence but also set the stage for higher levels of leadership.

Production – The Results Realm

Progressing to the Production level marks a significant shift in the leadership journey. Here, the leader's effectiveness is gauged not just by how they interact with their team (as in Permission), but by the tangible results they achieve. This level is characterized by the leader's ability to deliver outcomes that positively impact the organization's performance.

While Permission is about building relationships, Production is about achieving goals and generating momentum. The leader's influence at this stage is strengthened by their capacity to produce, to turn vision into reality. It's about setting targets, driving progress, and achieving key milestones. Leaders at this level are seen as effective and competent, as they bring about tangible improvements in productivity, sales, innovation, or other relevant measures of success.

Moving from Permission to Production requires a shift in focus. A leader must now balance the relational skills developed at the Permission level with the ability to set clear objectives, establish accountable standards, and drive the team toward achieving specific goals. It involves a deeper understanding of the business or project, strategic planning, and an ability to motivate and mobilize the team toward execution.

To facilitate this transition, leaders must:

1. Set Clear Goals: Define specific, measurable, achievable, relevant, and time-bound (SMART) objectives that align with the organization's vision.
2. Foster Accountability: Establish clear expectations and hold team members accountable for their contributions.
3. Empower Team Members: Delegate effectively and empower team members to take ownership of tasks and projects.
4. Lead by Example: Be a role model in terms of work ethic, commitment, and professional standards.
5. Encourage Initiative: Motivate the team to take initiative and be proactive in solving problems and pursuing opportunities.
6. Track and Measure Performance: Regularly review progress against goals and adjust strategies as needed.

At the Production level, a leader's success is directly linked to the success of their team. They earn respect not just through interpersonal skills but through their ability to lead the team to achieve real and meaningful results. This level of leadership is dynamic and impactful, solidifying the leader's credibility and setting the stage for further growth and influence.

People Development – The Reproduction Round
    The People Development level signifies a profound shift from focusing

on personal productivity to fostering the growth and development of others. At this stage, the leader transcends the achievement of organizational goals and delves into the realm of multiplying their influence by developing the capabilities and leadership potential in their team members.

This level is characterized by the leader's commitment to mentoring and coaching their subordinates. Leaders at the People Development level recognize that their success is no longer measured solely by what they can achieve individually, but by how effectively they can develop the skills, talents, and leadership potential of those around them. It's about building the next generation of leaders, thereby ensuring the long-term sustainability and success of the organization.

To move from Production to People Development, a leader must:

1. Shift Focus to Team Growth: Transition from a primary focus on achieving tasks and goals to prioritizing the growth and development of team members.
2. Invest Time in Others: Dedicate time and resources to mentor, coach, and train team members. This includes providing opportunities for learning, giving constructive feedback, and challenging them with new responsibilities.
3. Identify Potential Leaders: Recognize individuals within the team who show leadership potential and provide them with targeted development opportunities.
4. Foster a Learning Culture: Create an environment where continuous learning, experimentation, and personal development are encouraged and valued.
5. Delegate More Than Tasks: Go beyond assigning tasks; delegate authority and give team members the autonomy to make decisions. This helps in building their confidence and decision-making skills.

6. Lead by Inspiration: Inspire team members to envision their future roles and the impact they can have. Motivate them to aspire for leadership and guide them toward achieving those aspirations.
7. Model Leadership Qualities: Continue to demonstrate strong leadership qualities and be a role model in ethical behavior, commitment, and professionalism.

At the People Development level, the leader's influence is amplified through the successes and advancements of their team members. It is a testament to a leader's ability not just to lead but to inspire and empower others to lead as well. This level is about creating a legacy of leadership that transcends the individual and becomes a foundational part of the organization's culture.

Pinnacle – The Peak of Influence

Reaching the Pinnacle level is the epitome of leadership excellence. It is a stage where leaders are not just leading effectively within their own sphere but are influencing beyond their immediate environment. Leaders at the Pinnacle level have developed other leaders who are capable of leading, creating a multiplier effect that extends their influence far and wide. They are recognized not only for their accomplishments but also for the success of the leaders they have developed.

Transitioning to the Pinnacle level requires a leader to:

1. Cultivate a Legacy Mindset: Focus on building a lasting legacy. Leaders at this level think beyond their tenure and about the long-term impact of their leadership.
2. Embrace a Servant Leadership Philosophy: Prioritize the success and well-being of others. At the Pinnacle level, leadership is about serving and uplifting others, both within and outside the organization.

3. Continuously Develop and Mentor Leaders: Invest in raising new generations of leaders. This includes mentoring, inspiring, and guiding emerging leaders and helping them navigate their leadership journeys.

4. Demonstrate Visionary and Strategic Leadership: Show the ability to look ahead, anticipate changes, and prepare the organization and its leaders for future challenges and opportunities.

5. Maintain a Strong Personal Leadership Brand: Uphold a reputation of integrity, excellence, and effectiveness. A strong personal brand helps in influencing beyond the immediate circle.

6. Engage in Broader Community or Industry Leadership: Extend influence by taking on leadership roles in industry associations, community organizations, or public forums. This amplifies the leader's impact beyond their organization.

Staying at the Pinnacle level requires a continuous commitment to personal and professional growth, an ongoing effort to develop others, and a consistent demonstration of excellence in leadership. Leaders at this level are often seen as role models and thought leaders, influencing not only through direct interaction but also through the values, practices, and standards they have established.

The Pinnacle level is not just a position but a testament to a leader's lifelong commitment to leadership excellence. It's about having a transformational impact that transcends organizational boundaries and leaves an enduring imprint on the broader landscape of leadership. Leaders at this level are remembered not just for what they achieved, but for how they lifted others and shaped the future of leadership.

In summarizing the "5 Levels of Leadership" as outlined by John C. Maxwell, we see a clear trajectory of growth and influence in leadership.

The journey begins with a leader assuming a position of authority, often accompanied by a title that provides a platform for influence. However, true leadership extends far beyond the confines of a designated role. As leaders grow, they transition from relying on their positional power to earning the respect and trust of their team members. This shift marks the evolution from mere managers to inspirational figures who lead through empathy, understanding, and genuine concern for their team's welfare and growth.

At the higher echelons of leadership, the focus intensifies on achieving tangible results and fostering a culture of success. Leaders at these stages not only drive their teams toward organizational goals but also invest heavily in the development of future leaders. The pinnacle of this journey is reached when a leader's influence radiates beyond their immediate sphere, shaping the broader landscape of leadership. Here, the leader's impact is not measured by personal accomplishments but by the legacy they leave behind – a legacy characterized by a cadre of leaders who continue to propagate the values and vision instilled in them.

Throughout this progression, the constant is the leader's commitment to growth, both personally and for those around them. Maxwell's framework underscores the transformative power of effective leadership and the enduring impact it can have on individuals, organizations, and beyond. As leaders ascend these levels, they not only enhance their leadership capacities but also contribute significantly to the development of robust, resilient, and forward-looking leadership cultures.

"Extreme Ownership" by Jocko Willink and Leif Babin

I n "Extreme Ownership," authors Jocko Willink and Leif Babin draw from their extensive experience as Navy SEALs to present a compelling framework for leadership. The book is a comprehensive guide that encapsulates the lessons learned in high-stakes military environments and translates them into effective strategies for leaders in any sector. At its core, the book emphasizes the principle of Extreme Ownership, a philosophy where leaders take full responsibility for their team's performance, thus fostering an environment of discipline, decisiveness, and cohesive teamwork.

The concept of Extreme Ownership forms the bedrock of Jocko Willink and Leif Babin's leadership philosophy. It is a principle that insists on absolute responsibility for every aspect of team management and mission execution. At its core, Extreme Ownership means that a leader must own everything in their world, without excuse or blame. This foundational mindset is pivotal for any leader seeking to foster a culture of accountability, effectiveness, and success.

This doctrine is built on the premise that a leader, regardless of the circumstances, must always take responsibility for their team's failures as well as successes. It's a stance that eliminates any room for passing blame or shirking responsibilities, demanding instead that leaders confront challenges head-on, learn from mistakes, and continuously strive for improvement. This approach necessitates a high level of self-awareness, humility, and the courage to accept faults and learn from them.

The principle of Extreme Ownership is not just about taking responsibility for the outcomes but also about proactively leading the team through every phase of a mission or project. It involves detailed planning, clear communication, and unwavering commitment to the team's objectives. By embodying this principle, leaders set a powerful example for their team members, creating an environment where accountability is the norm, and every member is fully invested in the mission's success.

In this framework, leadership transcends the boundaries of mere oversight. It becomes an active, dynamic process where the leader is deeply involved in all facets of the team's operations, guiding, supporting, and driving them toward excellence. Extreme Ownership is a holistic approach, encompassing not just the strategic aspects of leadership but also the interpersonal dynamics that are crucial for team cohesion and morale.

This section of the book lays the groundwork for understanding how Extreme Ownership transforms the conventional approach to leadership, setting the stage for the exploration of its specific principles and their application in various contexts. It serves as a primer for the deeper insights that follow, each of which builds upon this fundamental concept to create a comprehensive leadership strategy.

Building upon the foundation of Extreme Ownership, Jocko Willink and Leif Babin introduce several key principles that are essential for effective leadership. These principles serve as guidelines for leaders to navigate the complexities of their roles while maintaining a focus on accountability and team success.

1. Belief in the Mission: For leaders to inspire their teams, they must first believe in the mission themselves. This belief is contagious and

crucial for garnering team commitment and enthusiasm. Leaders must understand and communicate the importance of the mission, aligning it with the team's values and goals.

2. Managing the Ego: A significant aspect of leadership is the ability to check one's ego. Ego can be a barrier to growth, learning, and collaboration. Leaders must foster humility and be open to feedback, placing the team's objectives above personal agendas or accolades.

3. Clear and Simple Communication: Effective leadership requires the ability to communicate plans and strategies clearly and concisely. Complexity can lead to confusion and errors, so simplifying messages ensures that every team member understands their role and the mission's objective.

4. Mutual Support - Cover and Move: This principle emphasizes teamwork and the importance of supporting one another. In military terms, "cover and move" translates to units covering each other while advancing. In a business context, it means departments or team members working together seamlessly toward a common goal, ensuring that no one is left struggling alone.

5. Prioritizing and Executing: Leaders often face multiple challenges and tasks. The ability to prioritize these effectively and then execute them decisively is crucial. This principle involves assessing the most pressing issues, delegating appropriately, and focusing resources where they are needed most to achieve success.

These key principles act as a compass for leaders, guiding them in creating and maintaining high-performing teams. They are intertwined with the concept of Extreme Ownership, as each principle reinforces the idea that leaders are ultimately responsible for their teams' outcomes. By embracing and applying these principles, leaders can navigate through challenges with confidence and clarity, driving their teams toward excellence and achievement.

In "Extreme Ownership," Jocko Willink and Leif Babin emphasize the importance of fostering effective team dynamics and the concept of decentralization in leadership. This approach is pivotal for building strong, agile teams that can operate efficiently and make decisions quickly, especially in high-pressure environments.

1. No Bad Teams, Only Bad Leaders: This powerful concept underlines the belief that the effectiveness of a team is largely dependent on the quality of its leadership. Willink and Babin argue that a skilled leader can transform even the most under performing teams into high achievers by instilling the principles of Extreme Ownership. The implication is clear: leaders must continuously evaluate and improve their leadership methods to elevate team performance.

2. Decentralized Command: Decentralization is a key strategy in SEAL operations, and it's equally effective in business. It involves empowering team members to make decisions and take action within their areas of responsibility. This requires trust in the team's abilities and clear communication of the mission's overall goals and boundaries. Decentralized command fosters initiative, flexibility, and rapid response, allowing teams to adapt quickly to changing circumstances.

3. Empowerment and Trust: For decentralization to be successful, leaders must develop a culture of empowerment and trust. This involves training team members to think independently and make sound decisions. It also means providing the necessary support and guidance without micromanaging, allowing individuals the freedom to apply their skills and judgment.

4. Leading Up and Down the Chain of Command: Effective team dynamics require leaders to communicate and lead both up and down the chain of command. This means not only directing subordinates

but also managing expectations and providing feedback to higher-ups. By ensuring that everyone, from the top of the organization to the bottom, understands the mission and their role in it, leaders can create a unified, cohesive effort toward achieving goals.

By focusing on effective team dynamics and decentralization, leaders following the Extreme Ownership model can build teams that are more than just the sum of their parts. Such teams are characterized by their resilience, adaptability, and capability to execute complex tasks efficiently under a variety of conditions. This approach not only enhances team performance but also contributes to the development of future leaders within the organization.

The principles of "Extreme Ownership" by Jocko Willink and Leif Babin, while rooted in military experience, are designed to be adaptable across a range of scenarios, particularly in business and organizational settings. This subsection explores how the concepts of Extreme Ownership can be applied and adapted to various contexts, enhancing leadership effectiveness and team success.

1. Adapting Military Principles to Business: The transition of principles from military to business environments is a key focus. In business, just as in the military, the fundamentals of leadership, such as decision-making, accountability, and team dynamics, remain constant. Leaders can apply these principles to drive operational efficiency, improve team cohesion, and enhance overall organizational performance.

2. Balancing Decisiveness and Flexibility: A critical aspect of applying Extreme Ownership is finding the right balance between being decisive and remaining flexible. In fast-paced and ever-changing business landscapes, leaders must make quick decisions while also being open to adapting their strategies as situations evolve. This

requires a keen understanding of the business environment and the agility to pivot when necessary.

3. Implementing in Diverse Organizational Structures: Extreme Ownership principles are versatile enough to be implemented in various organizational structures, from small startups to large multinational corporations. Leaders can tailor these principles to fit the unique culture, size, and goals of their organizations, ensuring that the leadership style and strategies are both effective and appropriate for their specific context.

4. Continuous Improvement and Leadership Development: Another key area is fostering an environment of continuous improvement and leadership development within teams and organizations. By embracing the principles of Extreme Ownership, leaders can encourage a culture of learning, where team members are constantly developing their skills and capabilities, thus preparing the organization for future challenges and opportunities.

In conclusion, the principles of Extreme Ownership are not limited to any single context but are broadly applicable across different industries and organizational models. The emphasis is on the adaptability of these principles and the importance of context in shaping how they are applied. Leaders who successfully adapt and apply these principles can lead their teams to greater heights of performance and achievement, regardless of the external environment or internal challenges they face.

"Start with Why" by Simon Sinek

This chapter introduces Simon Sinek's influential concept "Start with Why," a pivotal idea in understanding leadership and business strategy. Simon Sinek, an esteemed motivational speaker and author, advocates for the significance of identifying and articulating the core purpose or belief behind every action and decision in business and leadership. His insights stem from an exploration into what distinguishes the most successful and inspiring leaders and organizations, revealing that their common denominator is a clear and compelling 'Why' at the heart of their endeavors.

"Start with Why" delves into the essential question of what drives us, moving beyond the surface-level details of what we do and how we do it. Sinek's philosophy highlights the power of a well-defined 'Why' in crafting resonant leadership narratives, building influential brands, and fostering organizational cultures anchored in shared values. This chapter aims to explore the transformative impact of this concept in shaping effective leadership and creating businesses that not only succeed but also resonate deeply with their audiences.

Simon Sinek's Golden Circle concept is an insightful framework that delves into the essence of effective leadership and impactful business strategies. It features three concentric circles labeled 'Why', 'How', and 'What'. At its heart, 'Why' represents the purpose, cause, or belief that inspires and drives all actions. Surrounding this core are 'How', the specific actions or processes that realize the 'Why', and 'What', the tangible results or end products of these actions.

Contrary to the common approach of focusing on 'What' and then considering 'How', Sinek argues that the most inspiring leaders and successful organizations begin with 'Why'. This inside-out approach is critical – it signifies that compelling motivations and effective strategies are rooted in a clear understanding and articulation of purpose.

Through real-world examples, Sinek illustrates how organizations and leaders who prioritize their core purpose achieve remarkable success. A well-defined and inspiring 'Why' leads to distinctive and effective strategies, setting an entity apart in its field. When an organization's 'Why' is clear, the 'How' and 'What' naturally align, creating a coherent and powerful narrative. This approach not only captivates audiences but also fosters a loyal following, be it customers, employees, or other stakeholders.

Delving into the biological underpinnings of the 'Why' concept reveals its profound resonance with the human brain, particularly in how we respond to leadership and communication. The interaction between two main brain regions, the limbic and neocortex, is central to this understanding. The limbic brain, which processes feelings and emotions, is where the 'Why' resonates, while the neocortex is tasked with analytical and rational thought, handling the 'How' and 'What'.

This neurological framework is pivotal in grasping why messages starting with 'Why' often have a deeper impact. They engage the limbic brain, tapping into emotions and feelings, creating a level of engagement that rational arguments or factual data cannot achieve on their own. This emotional connection is a key driver in motivating and influencing human behavior, making it a crucial element in effective leadership.

Understanding the 'Biology of Why' sheds light on the varying impact of leadership and communication. It's not merely the content of the message that counts, but its ability to align with the emotional undercurrents of the audience. Leaders who grasp this biological aspect can shape their communication to resonate more profoundly with their teams or customers, fostering deeper relationships and prompting meaningful action. This insight underscores the importance of aligning the 'Why' with the human inclination toward emotionally charged messages, thereby blending science and strategy in the art of leadership.

The concept of 'Why' is not only a powerful tool for communication and motivation but also a fundamental element in building trust. By articulating and embodying their 'Why', leaders and organizations establish a sense of trust and forge loyal relationships with their customers and employees. This trust stems from a shared belief in the 'Why', a common purpose or set of values that resonate deeply with individuals.

When customers or team members believe in an organization's 'Why', they are not just buying a product or following instructions; they are aligning with a cause or a belief system. This forms the basis of the 'loyal customer' – someone who feels a strong, personal connection to the organization's purpose. Such loyalty goes beyond transactional relationships; it is rooted in emotional investment and a sense of shared identity.

For leaders, communicating the 'Why' effectively is crucial in cultivating this trust and loyalty. It involves more than just stating a mission statement; it requires authenticity, consistency, and a genuine demonstration of commitment to the core values and purpose. Leaders who successfully communicate their 'Why' create an environment where trust thrives and loyalty becomes a natural response.

This subsection highlights the transformative impact of 'Why' in creating and sustaining trust within an organization. It emphasizes how a well-articulated and authentic 'Why' can transcend the bounds of traditional business or team dynamics, fostering a culture where loyalty, commitment, and mutual trust become the defining characteristics of the relationship between leaders, their teams, and their customers.

The principle of 'Why' plays a pivotal role in effective leadership, particularly in its ability to inspire and motivate teams. Leaders who harness the power of 'Why' elevate their leadership beyond the mere execution of tasks or achievement of goals; they inspire a shared vision that resonates with the core values and beliefs of their team members.

Case studies of leaders who have successfully utilized the 'Why' in their leadership approach provide tangible examples of its effectiveness. These leaders stand out not just for their achievements but for the way they have inspired their teams and organizations to achieve collective success. Their ability to articulate a clear and compelling 'Why' aligns their team's efforts, motivates action and fosters a strong sense of belonging and purpose among members.

For leaders looking to harness the power of 'Why', the key lies in self-discovery and authentic expression. It requires introspection to understand one's driving purpose and the ability to articulate this 'Why' in a way that is both genuine and compelling. When leaders communicate their 'Why' effectively, they do more than direct actions; they inspire loyalty, ignite passion, and foster an environment where individuals are motivated to contribute not just their skills, but their commitment and enthusiasm to the shared mission.

This subsection emphasizes that the 'Why' is not a one-size-fits-all solution but a personal and unique driving force that, when effectively communicated, has the power to transform leadership from a position of authority to a role of inspiration and influence. It underscores the significance of 'Why' in shaping a leader's impact, driving team cohesion, and achieving lasting success.

In conclusion, Simon Sinek's "Start with Why" emphasizes the transformative impact of understanding and embodying one's core purpose in both leadership and business. This approach transcends conventional tactics by fostering deep resonance with teams and customers, enhancing loyalty, trust, and overall organizational success. Embracing 'Why' is more than a strategy; it's a pathway to genuine engagement, increased productivity, and the creation of a lasting legacy. This concept challenges leaders to introspect and align their actions with their fundamental beliefs, thereby cultivating an environment of authenticity and inspiration that propels both individuals and organizations toward sustained achievement and fulfillment.

"The Five Dysfunctions of a Team" by Patrick Lencioni

I n exploring the dynamics of team success and failure, Patrick Lencioni pinpoints five fundamental dysfunctions that commonly derail teams in various organizational contexts. These dysfunctions serve as a framework for diagnosing and resolving the complex issues that undermine team cohesion and effectiveness. By identifying these key areas – absence of trust, fear of conflict, lack of commitment, avoidance of accountability, and inattention to results – Lencioni provides both leaders and team members with insights into the deep-seated challenges that impede optimal team performance.

Lencioni's approach goes beyond identifying problems, offering practical solutions and strategies to overcome these obstacles. This exploration is crucial for any leader or team member seeking to build a strong, cohesive team. It's not just about recognizing what can go wrong in a team setting, but also about understanding how to foster an environment where trust, open communication, commitment, accountability, and a focus on collective goals are the norm. This sets the stage for teams to not only achieve their objectives but to excel and thrive in their collaborative efforts.

The foundation of a high-functioning team is trust, and its absence is the first dysfunction that Lencioni identifies. A lack of trust within a team typically stems from a reluctance to show vulnerability among team members. When individuals are unwilling to open up and expose their weaknesses or mistakes, it leads to an environment where trust cannot flourish.

Trust is more than just believing that team members will fulfill their tasks. It's about creating a space where vulnerability is not only accepted but encouraged. This type of trust allows for honest and open communication, creating a bedrock for strong teamwork. Without it, teams are likely to fall into patterns of guarded behavior and missed opportunities for genuine collaboration.

Building trust requires intentional efforts from all team members, especially leaders. It involves fostering an atmosphere where individuals feel safe to express their thoughts, admit their mistakes, and ask for help. This often means leaders need to lead by example, showing their vulnerabilities and encouraging others to do the same. Trust-building exercises and regular, candid discussions can also play a significant role in overcoming this dysfunction. Once a foundation of trust is established, teams are better positioned to engage in healthy conflict, commit to decisions, hold one another accountable, and focus on achieving collective results.

The second dysfunction in Lencioni's framework is the fear of conflict, a common issue where teams shy away from open, constructive debate. This avoidance often stems from a desire to maintain artificial harmony, leading to situations where important issues are not addressed, and decisions are made without thorough discussion.

Healthy conflict is essential for the growth and progress of any team. It allows for diverse perspectives to be aired and debated, leading to more robust solutions. Teams that fear conflict often resort to passive-aggressive behaviors, backchannel discussions, or worse, complete silence on critical matters. This avoidance can stifle innovation and prevent the team from fully exploring options and making well-informed decisions.

To overcome the fear of conflict, teams need to cultivate an environment where differing opinions are not just tolerated but encouraged. Leaders play a crucial role in setting this tone. They need to demonstrate that conflict can be constructive and is a vital part of the team's process. Encouraging open discussions, actively soliciting differing views, and managing these discussions to stay focused on issues rather than personal attacks are key strategies. By normalizing and managing healthy conflict, teams can move beyond superficial agreement, fostering a culture of deep engagement and collaborative problem-solving.

The third dysfunction identified by Lencioni is a lack of commitment, often arising from ambiguous decision-making and a failure to achieve clarity and buy-in. This dysfunction occurs when team members, having not openly aired their opinions and concerns, end up half-heartedly supporting team decisions. The absence of clear direction and commitment can lead to confusion, decreased morale, and subpar execution.

Teams suffering from this dysfunction often find themselves revisiting decisions repeatedly, leading to inefficiencies and frustration. A key factor contributing to this lack of commitment is the absence of healthy conflict, as discussed earlier. When team members do not feel their voices are heard or their viewpoints considered, their commitment to team decisions and outcomes wanes.

To counter this dysfunction, leaders need to foster an environment where all team members feel their input is valued and considered. This involves encouraging open dialogue and ensuring that all viewpoints are discussed before reaching a decision. Importantly, once a decision is made, it needs to be communicated and committed to by the entire team, even by those who initially disagreed. This commitment doesn't necessarily require consensus but rather a collective effort to move forward with the agreed-upon plan. Clarity of purpose, transparency in decision-making, and a unified front in execution are crucial steps in overcoming the dysfunction of a lack of commitment.

The fourth dysfunction, avoidance of accountability, occurs when team members are reluctant to call out peers on performance or behaviors that might be detrimental to the team. This often stems from a desire to avoid interpersonal discomfort, leading to a culture where mediocrity is tolerated and the team's overall standards decline.

In a team where accountability is avoided, members may see underperformance but choose not to address it, either because they expect someone else to do it or because they fear damaging relationships. This lack of accountability can create a burden on team leaders and demotivate members who are committed and performing well.

To combat this dysfunction, it's crucial to establish a culture where holding each other accountable is seen as an essential part of team dynamics. This requires clear communication of expectations and standards from the outset. Leaders should encourage and model direct and respectful feedback, making it a regular part of team interactions. Additionally, establishing clear goals and defined roles helps in creating a sense of personal responsibility among team members.

Creating a sense of mutual accountability also involves recognizing and celebrating achievements, as well as addressing issues promptly and constructively. When team members understand that accountability is about maintaining high standards for the collective success of the team, and not just pointing out faults, it becomes easier to address issues openly and effectively.

The final dysfunction in Lencioni's model is inattention to results, where team members prioritize their own personal status or ego above the collective goals of the team. This dysfunction is often the culmination of the other four dysfunctions, manifesting in a lack of focus on what the team needs to achieve together.

When team members are not committed to a common set of outcomes or when individual agendas take precedence, the team's performance suffers. This lack of focus on results can lead to complacency, stagnation, and a failure to achieve key objectives. Team members might focus on their career advancement, personal recognition, or even the success of their sub-teams, rather than the success of the entire team.

Overcoming this dysfunction requires a shift in perspective where the team's results are viewed as paramount. Leaders play a crucial role in instilling this mindset. They need to set clear, measurable goals that are understood and accepted by all team members. Regularly reviewing these goals and the team's progress toward them helps in maintaining focus and alignment.

Creating a culture where team achievements are celebrated, and individual contributions are recognized as part of the broader success can help realign members' priorities. By emphasizing the importance of collective outcomes and holding the team accountable for achieving them, leaders can ensure that the team's efforts are fully directed toward reaching its shared goals.

In sum, Patrick Lencioni's "The Five Dysfunctions of a Team" provides a comprehensive guide to identifying and addressing the key challenges that hinder team effectiveness. Each dysfunction - absence of trust, fear of conflict, lack of commitment, avoidance of accountability, and inattention to results - builds upon the previous one, creating a layered understanding of how teams can fail or succeed. This model serves as a valuable tool for leaders and team members alike, offering insights into the dynamics of team interaction and the essential elements of a strong, cohesive team.

Addressing these dysfunctions is not a one-time fix but an ongoing process of development and improvement. It requires a commitment from all team members to engage openly, communicate effectively, commit wholeheartedly to decisions, hold each other accountable, and focus unwaveringly on collective outcomes. By actively working on these aspects, teams can enhance their performance, foster a positive and productive environment, and achieve their objectives more efficiently and effectively. Understanding and applying the principles outlined in "The Five Dysfunctions of a Team" is crucial for any team aiming to unlock its full potential and achieve lasting success.

Conclusion

In wrapping up this exploration into leadership, it's evident that the art of leading is both complex and dynamic, demanding continuous adaptation and learning. The journey through these pages has not only highlighted the multifaceted nature of leadership but also emphasized its critical role in shaping progress and inspiring change. Leadership is more than a set of skills; it's a mindset, an approach to life and work that sets the tone for success and innovation.

This journey has underscored the importance of continuous learning in leadership. Like any refined craft, leadership demands diligence, introspection, and a commitment to perpetual growth. Through the lens of some of the most insightful leadership books, we have ventured into the minds of great leaders and thinkers, gaining access to a wealth of knowledge and experience. These books serve as a guiding light, offering invaluable perspectives and tools that are essential for navigating the complexities of modern leadership.

As you reflect on the insights from each chapter, consider this book as your compass in the vast ocean of leadership literature. The selected works are more than just informative; they are transformative, each offering unique wisdom that is crucial for meeting the evolving challenges of leadership. They prompt a redefinition of conventional perspectives, encouraging you to think more broadly, act with conviction, and lead with a renewed sense of purpose.

Embarking on this literary journey marks a pivotal step in your leadership development. It invites you to challenge your assumptions, embrace bold new strategies, and lead with a vision that transcends the ordinary. This is not just an end but a beginning, a point from which to launch into deeper exploration and continued transformation in your leadership journey.

References

1. Nahavandi, Afsaneh. (2014). "The Art and Science of Leadership." 7th Edition. Pearson.
2. Maxwell, John C. (2011). "The 5 Levels of Leadership: Proven Steps to Maximize Your Potential." Center Street.
3. Willink, Jocko, and Babin, Leif. (2015). "Extreme Ownership: How U.S. Navy SEALs Lead and Win." St. Martin's Press.
4. Sinek, Simon. (2009). "Start with Why: How Great Leaders Inspire Everyone to Take Action." Portfolio.
5. Lencioni, Patrick. (2002). "The Five Dysfunctions of a Team: A Leadership Fable." Jossey-Bass.
6. OpenAI. (2023). ChatGPT [Large language model].